Facebook Ads

Build Your Brand with Facebook Advertising.

Randall Kadner

CONTENTS

Introduction

Facebook, the biggest social network in the world, is a part of the daily routine for a good majority of the world's population. Many of the people close to us check their Facebook accounts the moment they wake up, before they end their day and all of the time in between. Because it attracts the attention of billions of people every single day, it can be used as an effective marketing tool for businesses.

In fact, many major corporations have slowly integrated their Facebook (and other social networks) marketing into their regular marketing routine. Many small businesses around the world also depend on it to attract new and return customers alike.

If your own company or organization has not taken the plunge of marketing on Facebook, this is your chance. Gone are the days when you only need to make a business page to make your brand visible in the social network. Facebook no longer give away its users' attention for free. To support their free platform, they encourage both small and large businesses to use Facebook Ads.

If the idea of using online ads sounds daunting to you, don't worry. Facebook makes it easier for you to learn online advertising skills which are requisite to getting started. In fact, they will even provide you with the images that you might need to make your ads more attractive.

Let Facebook advertising be your first step into the world of paid online marketing. More than 90 percent of businesses on Facebook actually do not use paid promotions. It often takes these "organic" marketers years to develop their business page and convert their social media following into actual sales.

Online marketing does not need to be a slow and difficult process. However, if done correctly, your Facebook Ads can generate sales, new signups, or any other type of conversion for your business with an instant. This book will guide you on how you can create your first Facebook ad. Here, we will discuss how you can use Facebook Ads to further boost your business' performance online. The book also talks about the pitfalls that you should avoid when you are creating your first ad campaigns and the best practices that you must observe.

Using this book, you will learn not to rely on distracting metrics in your campaigns. The goal of any marketing campaign is to convert people from being audiences to becoming customers of a business or to take part in the activities of an organization. Likes and impressions alone do not fulfill this criteria. This book teaches you to avoid falling for this so-called "vanity metrics". It teaches you to focus more of your effort and attention on the real goals of your company or organization. If your Facebook ads cannot get conversions for your organization, consider adjusting your strategies to drive more sales or to acquire more signups.

At the end of the day, Facebook Advertising is a skill that needs to be developed over time. You need to learn before you can succeed. This book provides you with the informational tools to hasten that learning process.

Chapter One: Understanding Social Media

For you to properly develop a Facebook Ad campaign, you first need to learn what social media is and what makes Facebook the best social network for you.

What are Social Networks?

Social networks refer to websites and mobile applications that allow users to create and share content. The main purpose of most social networking platforms is to facilitate social interactions for users all over the world. Through these platforms, users can interact not only with their friends and family members, but also with strangers from different countries.

Social networks are a subset of the broader term: social media. While social media includes vlogs, blogs, entertainment and news websites, social networks refer to the part of social media that encourages social interactions. Facebook, Twitter, Instagram, Snapchat and LinkedIn all fall in this category.

Facebook is one of the most successful social networks in the world today. There is no simple way to explain what Facebook is because it has so many features. Each person has an option on what feature they want to spend their time on. To understand how your ads will be shown on the Facebook platform, you will need to learn how your own audience interacts when they are logged in.

What makes Facebook successful as a social network?

The users make Facebook the success that it is today. Facebook attracts more than 2.2 billion users every month from all over the world. Because Facebook is such a useful networking tool, these active users keep coming back on a daily basis. In June 2018, Facebook reported that an average of 1.4 billion people logged onto the app or the website every day. This means that more than half of Facebook's active users log into the platform daily.

User activity can vary from creating status posts to uploading media files like photos and videos. According to Gizmodo, Facebook users upload around 300 million photos daily. Even more status updates and comments are created every day.

Every person's activity on the platform can be a source of data for the social media giant. Aside from uploads, status updates, and comments, Facebook has other features that allow it to collect data even from passive users.

Passive users refer to people who just lurk in the social network. These users do not post as much content in their accounts. However, Facebook can still gather data from them through the types of posts that they interact with.

"Reactions" are a set of emoji that users can use to passively react to a piece of content in the platform. As of the writing of this book, there are six options for this feature: Love (the heart emoji), Ha-ha, Wow, Sad, Angry and the Like (thumbs-up).

Aside from these emoji, data can also be collected from Facebook Messenger. Messenger is Facebook's email/chat feature. Users can use it to talk privately and to share media files. Many businesses also use Messenger as their primary real-time customer service tool.

Is it the right platform for your business?

In terms of user demographics, Facebook is most popular towards the 25-35 age range. This subset makes up 29.7% of the active users. This age range is what most marketing experts refer to as the millennial generation. In the US, around 50% of 18-24 year-olds also use Facebook daily.

These two age groups are important because they are the future spenders in the platform. These two age groups are the first generations of the so-called "internet natives". They are used to consuming online content and they are open to new opportunities online that your ads may present.

That said, you should do research on your own potential customers to learn if Facebook ads is the right option for you. While Facebook statistically dwarfs other social networks in terms of daily active users, not all of them are responsive towards ads. Unlike search engine users, the people on Facebook aren't looking for anything specific. Most of them are there to kill time and interact with their friends and family. It is safe to say that the majority of these users are not always in the mood for buying.

This does not mean that Facebook ads are less effective as a marketing platform. It only means that you will need to employ the right strategy to make users engage with your ads. You will need to capture their attention.

Facebook's Best Features

To understand the different strategies that will be discussed in the later chapters of this book, you first need to understand how users interact with the Facebook platform. Here are some of the important features in Facebook that you should focus on when advertising:

- Facebook Newsfeed

The Facebook Newsfeed is one of the most important features for marketers. When a person logs into their account, they are first directed to their newsfeed. In the newsfeed, the users will see a list of content shared by their friends and the pages they follow. They will also see content shared in the Facebook groups that they are members of.

You can think of the Newsfeed as Facebook's content delivery system. It is the part of a person's account where Facebook aggregates content for the user to interact with. Each piece of content in the newsfeed is called a "post".

A user has multiple options for engaging with content in their newsfeed. The most passive way of engagement is the reaction emoji options. The user can react to a content in their newsfeed using one of the six emoji discussed earlier most commonly with a "like".

If users have something to say about the content, they also have the option to post a comment below the content. By default, most of the comments are hidden. A user will need to click on the comment link to show all of the comments on the related post.

Lastly, users have the option to share the posts they see on their newsfeed. When they share posts, they are basically showing it to their own friends and followers via their "wall" or alternatively through the private messaging system "messenger".

As a marketer, you are obviously aiming for your content to show in the newsfeeds of your followers. In the past, posts from pages were shown organically (without pay). However, things have changed as more and more businesses participate in Facebook marketing. The increased level of competition makes it almost impossible for content from business pages to show in the user newsfeed organically.

- The Timeline and Profile Information

The Facebook timeline can be found in the profile page of an individual user. This part of their profile shows the content they shared publicly on Facebook. The contents are usually arranged chronologically.

For marketers, the Facebook timeline is a great tool for studying the people who follow their Facebook pages. When creating a Facebook Ad campaign a marketer can check the timeline of some of their followers to check for demographical data to target.

- Business Pages

There are two types of profile pages within Facebook. The first type is the individual user page. This is the personal type of profile page and it is meant to represent a real person. Business pages on the other hand, represents business entities. They are just like personal pages with some added features.

One of the biggest differences is that business pages cannot add Facebook "friends". Instead, users can only like a business page to show that they support the business it represents. Some users can also follow a page. Following allows the content shared by the business page to show in the newsfeeds of the user.

While content posted in business pages are not as effective in reaching the newsfeeds as they used to be, you should still create a business page within Facebook. If you have one, it will be easier for potential customers to find your business and funnel them into other platforms.

On your business page, potential customers will be able to find all the basic information about your business. It may contain your business address, your website URL and link, other socials, your phone number and even your business hours. Each business page comes with a page description. In this section, you can tell people what your business is about.

Your business page can also serve as a tool for letting current customers know what's new with your business. You can use your business page's timeline by creating posts about your most current promotions that your customers may like, or providing followers with value giving them reason to further supporting your business.

- Facebook Groups

The Facebook Group feature is also an effective way of getting attracting likeminded people towards your business. Contents posted or shared to Facebook

Groups can effectively reach the newsfeeds of the members. If your business has a potential to get return customers, you should consider creating a Group for your loyal customers.

In a Facebook Group, users can interact with each other about a certain topic. It is common for example, for fans of sports teams to create Facebook Groups to connect with other fans. In the Group, they discuss topics that are within their interest and they can expect replies and reactions from likeminded people.

Using Groups as a business tool can be tricky. However, if you successfully find a way to attract the right types of users to become a member of a Facebook Group, you should be able to increase the reach of your organic posts and your promotions.

Chapter Two: Starting with Facebook Pages

If you have done your research and you are convinced that Facebook ads will give you an edge in your business niche, it's time to create your Facebook ad account.

Creating your Business Page

As discussed in the previous chapter, your business needs a business page to start advertising on Facebook. There are two ways to create a business page. Even without a Facebook account, you can find a "Create a Page" link on the Facebook.com log in page.

If you are already logged into your Facebook account, you can also create one by clicking on the menu button. This can be found in the upper right corner of your Facebook app on your mobile phone. It looks like three lines stacked on top of one another. For desktop, the menu button looks like a dropdown arrow in the upper right corner of the screen.

Choose between "Business or Brand" and "Community or Public Figure"

After clicking on the "Create a Page" link, you will be given an option to choose between "Business or Brand" and "Community or Public Figure". It's best to choose the Business or Brand option because it contains all the features you need to start an advertising campaign. Click on the "Get Started" link to continue.

Input your Business Name

For the next step, you will be asked to provide a page name. Make sure that you use your business name and that you check it for proper spelling. This is because you will only have a few opportunities to change your page name so it's best to get it right the first time. If your business acts as a branch of a bigger business chain, you may want to add your location to the page name.

In the same step, you will also need to add the category of your business. Just start typing the category of your business and Facebook will start suggesting canned categories to you. Choose among the preset categories. If you are satisfied with the name and the category of your business, click on the "Continue" button.

Add a Profile Picture and a Cover Photo

The profile picture of your business page should help Facebook users remember your business. If you already have a business logo, you could use it in this step. The ideal size is 360 x 360 pixels. If you have an available image, you can upload it at this stage. If not, you can opt to skip this step and upload the profile picture later.

The cover photo is a rectangular image that appears at the back of your profile photo. If you choose to use your business logo as your profile photo, you could use an image of your best-selling or newest product as your cover photo. This way, your users will be able to guess what your business is about just by looking at your business name, your profile photo and your cover photo. These three will be the first page features that they will see when they check your business page.

After these steps, your Business Page is ready for viewing. However, it would be best to make sure that your page is completed properly before actually sharing it with other people. Here are some of the actions that you will need to take to complete your business page:

Edit Page Info

Very few of your potential customers will actually go to your page info. Nevertheless, you should still complete the information required in this section of your page for those who do bother to check it.

When using a desktop, you will be able to find this option just below the cover photo in your page's home page. When you click on the "Edit Page Info" button, a pop-up form will appear where you will be able to edit information like your page's category, the impressum, the page's contact details, and your business' physical location and your business hours. The contact details and your location are both important if your goal is to make Facebook users go to your brick-and-mortar store.

In the contact details section, you will be able to add your business phone number, your website and your email address. It's ideal to fill these details out before you even consider creating your first ad copy.

Create a Username

The username is a shortened version of your page name. A username makes it easier for your fans to tag your page whenever they have a post that mentions your business. Pick a username that's easy to spell and remember. It should also be related to the name of your page. You can find the link for this option just below the username.

Create a Call-to-Action Button for your Page

The call-to-action button of your page can be found below your cover photo. This is a button that will lead users to the goal of your Facebook marketing campaign when pressed. As of the writing of this book, these are the available call-to-actions:

- Book Now
- Contact Us
- Learn More
- Shop Now
- Use App

Connect your Facebook Page with your other Social Network Accounts

Facebook also gives you the option to connect your other social media accounts to your Facebook business page. You will be able to do this by going to the About Page and clicking on the "Edit Other Accounts". You will then see a pop-up form that you can use to add accounts from other social networks such as Twitter, Instagram, Snapchat, YouTube and Twitch. You can add as many accounts as you need.

Creating your first posts

Now that your business page is up and running, it's time to start networking. The first step is to add content to your page so that people can see what you have to offer when they decide to visit it. To add posts to your Facebook page, go to your page's timeline (in the Home Page or the Posts Page) and click on the text box that says "Write a Post".

You have the option to add photos, a video or a text post. Both photos and videos can be accompanied with a text description. Ideally, you want to keep your timeline exciting by posting different types of media.

In the beginning, make it a habit to create at least one post a day. You can post photos of your current products on your Facebook page to remind people of your business. If you have special promotions, you should also post details for it during the hours when your clients are likely to be online.

Facebook makes it easy for page administrators to maintain their online pages. One important feature that you will surely find useful is the option to schedule your post to be published on a later date. This a great feature for experimenting on the performance of posting during different parts of the day.

Invite friends who may be interested in your business

Facebook pages are excellent tools for increasing the effects of word-of-mouth marketing. If one of your fans shares a post, at least 4 of his or her friends will see that post. They, in turn, may choose to spread the word further by sharing the same content. This is how content become viral in social media. To harness the power of Facebook when it comes to creating buzz for your business, you need to begin encouraging people to "like" your page. By doing so, some of your posts will be shown in their personal newsfeeds.

To do this, you may choose to start with your Facebook friends. Facebook gives you the option to invite your friends to like the page in the sidebar of your page. You may find this in the sidebar box labelled "Know friends who might like your Page?" To start inviting friends, just write the name of the

Facebook friend that you wish to invite in the search box provided. Next, click on the "Invite" button. This will send a notification to the user with an invitation to like your page.

In this page, most beginners would invite all of their friends. While this may seem like a good idea, it's best not to use the same strategy. Instead, you should only ask your friends who are truly interested on your business to like your page. The number of likes on your page does really matter. Instead, you want to focus more on the engagement of your fans on your content. If most of your fans do not interact on your page, the Facebook algorithm will no longer show your content in users' newsfeeds. Because of this, it's better to have only a few engaged fans than hundreds of passive fans.

By posting new content daily and encouraging engagement from your users, you will be able to spark the interest of potential customers.

Chapter Three: Creating Your First Facebook Ad

Facebook makes it easy for you to make ads from your Facebook business page. They also have different options for promotion that you can choose from. The best ad option for you will depend on the type of business goal you have for your Facebook marketing campaign.

Setting Your Ad Goals

The general strategy when setting Facebook ad goals is to align your ad goals to your real-world business goals. If your immediate business goal is to set more appointments, you could use your Facebook audience as a source of new leads. If your business goal is to sell more stuff, you can also use your Facebook ads to do this.

Just like with any marketing endeavor, your Facebook marketing campaign will be limited by the amount of time and funding you can pump into it. You want to keep your campaign efficient and effective to make sure that the Facebook marketing campaign will lead to real-world successful results.

To make sure that your Facebook campaign is aligned with your business goals, write those goals down before you even make an ad. Your written goals will make decision making easier as you go through the succeeding steps.

Now that you have a goal for your campaign, you will need to choose the best way to measure success. Facebook provides various measurable objectives. The check these ad objectives, go to the Facebook Ads Manager page:

https://www.facebook.com/adsmanager/creation

(Note: You must be logged-in to Facebook to access this page)

In the creation page of the Facebook Ad Manager, you will see three categories of objectives: Awareness, Consideration and Conversion.

- **Awareness Campaigns**

If your business goal is Awareness, Facebook will track the number of people who sees your page (Reach). The ads will be optimized to maximize this number.

Awareness is not always a good business goal because it does not really bring any immediate return on your investment. There is also no guarantee that the people who see your ad will be converted into regular customers. Because of this, ads with Awareness objectives tend to be cheaper than those with other types of objectives.

- ## Consideration Campaigns

When people are already familiar with your business, they may consider to do more active responses towards your ads. The consideration objective allows your ads to measure one of the following metrics:

- *Traffic to a website*
- *Content engagement (reactions, comments and shares)*
- *App installs*
- *Video view*
- *Lead generation*
- *Messages*

If your business process makes use of any of these steps, you may choose that option as your ad campaign objective. While awareness campaigns are optimized for views, consideration campaigns are optimized for users to take a desired action. Because this kind of ad goal requires action from users, its costs tend to be higher than those of awareness campaigns.

- ## Conversion Campaigns

Lastly, we have conversion campaigns. This type of campaign objective will lead to actions from users that can eventually lead to actual returns for the business. You can create three types of conversion campaigns:

- *Website or App conversions*

Website or app conversions refer to actions that users need to take through your website or app. If you have an ecommerce store for example, you can use this type of objective to track sales that came directly from Facebook. You will need to attach a Facebook Pixel code in select pages in your website to be able to track this objective.

Aside from sales, you can also use this objective to track downloads, increase email subscriptions and many other website or app activities.

- *Catalog Sales*

If you have a published product catalogue on your Facebook page, you can use the Catalog Sales objective to measure the number of sales you've made in your catalogue. With this type of objective, your campaign would be optimized to help increase the likelihood of users purchasing from your online store. For you to be able to use this campaign objective, you should already have an active catalog on your page. To create one, just go to the Facebook catalog management page:

https://www.facebook.com/products

- *Store Visits*

Many small businesses who are starting out on Facebook would much rather encourage their Facebook fans to visit their brick-and-mortar stores. If this is the case for your business, you might want to use the Store Visit objective with your campaign.

Setting Your Campaign Budget

You can easily create ads on Facebook using a budget as small as a dollar a day. If this is your first campaign, make sure that you use only the minimum amount of money. Why? This is because no one gets the targeting right on their first try. When the first ad goes live, it is common for beginners to realize that they made some sort of mistake and that adjustments need to be made. To prevent losing a big chunk of your budget, try to keep your budget low while you're still in the testing phase. Only commit a bigger chunk of your budget if you are more confident with your audience targeting.

Ad Campaign Types in Facebook

- **Content Boost**

Content boost is a type of promotion that allows page owners to directly promote the content posted on their respective pages. If you own a page, you will have the boost button available at the bottom of the page. It will open a pop-up window that allows you to set the targeting criteria, the budget and the duration.

Content boosts are a quick and easy way to get some of your most important content out there. Without a content boost, many of your fans will not see your posts since they tend to get buried under newer ones after a day. With content boost, they will be able to find and see your posts even if they haven't logged in for a while.

While boosting content can be effective, it needs to be done selectively. It is best to allow a post to stay on your page for 24 hours before actually boosting it. This way, your post will get some engagement from your fans organically first. After getting 20-50 reactions, you can choose to boost the post. Doing this usually increases its reach and the overall effectiveness of the boosted post.

Boosted posts get the most clicks when they are designed according to the interests of the target audience. Because this type of promotion can be generated fast, some marketers do become impulsive when using it. This usually happens when they do not see their expected amount of engagement on their organic posts.

As a rule of thumb, try to avoid making decisions on the fly. You can do this by making a post plan. In the plan, identify the posts that you plan on boosting. Don't just boost post because you think it is entertaining. Instead, only boost posts that actually contributes to the main objective of your post or your organization. Even with boosted posts, you need to identify a conversion task.

- **Page Promotion**

A Page Promotion is type of ad campaign that is meant to get more likes for your Facebook page. After creating the page and asking the people you know to like and follow the page, you will eventually experience a slowdown in the growth of the fan base of the page. This is normal and you should not worry about it. If your organization requires social proof, you can use Page Promotion to increase the number of likes in a short period.

Aside from that reason however, Page Promotion has no direct business value. Its primary goal is to make people like your page. Likes however, are considered as no more than _vanity metrics_ by most marketers. If only a small percentage of your fans actually engage with your content, you will not get real world conversions like sales or signups.

Only use Page Promotion if you are pressured to increase the number of likes or engagement in a particular post. However, do not include it in your long term ad campaign plan. The number of fans on your page will naturally increase as you keep it active through regular posts and ad campaigns.

- **Lead Generation**

Lead generation refers to process of making people subscribe for a service or to volunteer. Many organizations use lead generation campaigns to attract Facebook users into their organization.

Lead generation generally does not require any financial commitment from the user. Instead, it asks for personal information that some people may not be comfortable to give.

Lead generation ad campaigns are effective for companies that require actual human contact before they can make a sale. Companies that sell big ticket items and services like cars, homes, and insurance policies need this kind of ad campaign.

Before you actually start doing a lead generation ad, make sure that you know what you'll be using the collected data for. One common step that sales professional do is to follow up on the leads through a phone call, an email or a Facebook private message. The general goal of the follow-up message is to set up a sales meeting. The effectiveness of as lead generation campaign depends on how effective the follow-up process is.

- **Website/ App Visitors**

The next general type of Facebook campaign is the website or app visitor campaign. This the most difficult type of campaign to pull off because it requires the users to actually click out the Facebook platform and perform a task. It is also the most financially rewarding if you are able to successfully convert people at a low cost per conversion.

This type of campaign has two steps. The first step is to make people click on your ad on Facebook without getting any bounced visitors. You will need a tested and proven ad copy for this step to be successful. Unfortunately, there is no other way to test your ad copies other than to do actual ad campaigns.

The next step is to convert your users in the website outside of Facebook. You success in this step will depend on the effectiveness of your landing page outside of Facebook. Ideally, you want to convert them on that landing page. You will lose some of your prospect customers if the process requires them to click away from the landing page.

The Anatomy of a Facebook Ad

Unlike other types of ads online, Facebook is strict when it comes to the way ads on their network are shown. You will need to work with the basic Facebook ad template if you wish to advertise in the social network.

- Suggested or Sponsored Content Disclaimer

Most Facebook ads start with a header that says "Suggested Post" or "Sponsored". This is an ad disclaimer and in most cases, it is the only thing separating ads from looking like real posts. Aside from the Sponsored label, the other parts of the ads are very similar to your average Facebook post.

- Header

On the header portion of the ad, you will see the name of the advertiser. This is where your business name will go. Just like with a Facebook post, you will see the profile picture of the business page at the upper left of the ad post, followed by the name of the page. There might also be an additional "Sponsored" label below the name of the advertiser.

- Like Page Call-to-Action

Directly opposite to the name of the advertiser is a call-to-action. It could say "Like Page" or something similar. This is common among all sidebar and mobile apps.

- Post Description

Below the header line, you will see a short description. Facebook encourages advertisers to keep the description short. The text limit is 90 characters. The idea is to create short but attention-grabbing intros and a call to action texts. If you have an ongoing promotion, this is where you can explain to potential clients exactly what you are offering. However, you need to keep things informative yet concise or you will run out of characters.

- Post Image

Facebook provides advertisers with stock images to fill the image space. Ideally though, you should have your own image that fits the nature and the message of your campaign.

It is important to remember that Facebook ads have a 20% text limit. When you submit an image to Facebook, it divides that image into 10 squares. If the text portion of your image occupies more than 2 squares out of the 10, the Facebook image will be rejected. It's better if you keep the text size below 20% of the area of the image.

The image is the main attention grabber of your ad. You will need to test multiple images to see which ones work best in attracting the desired type of engagement from the audience.

- The Link's Meta Title and Description

When creating an ad, Facebook will ask you for a link that would lead any user who clicks on it to your website. If you write a valid URL, Facebook will fetch the Title and the Meta Description of the landing page. Don't worry because you can still change this manually with the ad editor.

- Domain Name and the Ad Call-to-Action Button

Below the meta-information, you should be able to see the domain name where the ad link is leading to. Many Facebook ads are linked to the Facebook page of the advertiser. In this case, the domain name that will be written in the bottom will be Facebook.com or simply Facebook in narrow devices.

Directly across the domain name, you should be able to see the Call-to-Action button specific for the ad. This call to action reflects the objective of the ad. If your ad's objective is to gain more likes for the Facebook Page, the Call-to-Action button should say "Like Page". If the objective is to get more website membership, the button may say "Sign Up".

Chapter Four: Choosing Your Audience

Now that you are familiar with the basics of using Facebook ads, it's time to talk about the Facebook's ad targeting technology. This feature makes Facebook ads unique from other advertising platforms. Google Ads uses search queries and the person's search history for targeting their ads. However, aside from these information, the search giant actually has a limited information about the users interacting with their ad network. This is the reason why we often see mismatched ads when using Google.

Facebook ads aim to fix this. Facebook has a lot of raw information about their users. Just by signing up, they will know your age, name, location and email address. Most companies would go to great lengths to get these information from their target market. Facebook, however, takes it a bit further. The moment you start adding friends, Facebook's AI algorithm is able to associate certain characteristics with your account. The more you interact with the system, the more information the ad algorithm has on you. This lets the ad targeting technology know what types of ads will likely work for you.

Every user on Facebook is profiled in a similar way. The social network giant keeps track of all the things you like and don't like. They keep track of the posts that made you unfollow certain people and pages.

This is great news for marketers. Because of Facebook's meticulous data gathering, we can be rest assured that our ads will be shown to the correct people. It's just a matter of getting your targeting setting right. Let's begin with learning about the targeting options available for Facebook ads:

Here are some of the audience demographic information that you should focus on first:

- **Age group**

The age group and your market's location are the two most important information that you need to consider. You want to keep your targeting to just the right amount of audience to make sure that you are not wasting money on unwanted views. By limiting your ads to show only to a specific age group, you make sure that only people who are interested in your product will see your ad. This is particularly important if you are selling a product or service that is more likely to be bought by young and middle-aged adults.

If this is the case, you do not want your ads to show up in the screens of people who are too young. These people may not be interested in the product or service you are offering. These views will only be wasted when shown to lower age groups.

By controlling the age range of your ad targeting, you are also making sure that your ad is only shown to people who have the money to buy your product or service. While Facebook users can range from 13 and up, you must filter your views to users who are older than 18 years old. Most users who are in the 18 to 22 age range do not have a lot of disposable income yet, especially for luxurious items. If your product is on the expensive side, you may want to make sure that you target only the people who are capable of paying for it.

The best age range to target fall in the 25-32 age range. People in this age range are more likely to be employed with no parental commitments yet. They are more open to spending on less important things. People aged between 30 and 40 are likely to be starting out a family. If your product or service is related to this life milestone, you may want to limit your ad targeting to this age group. This includes products such as homeware, small homes, second hand cars and family related insurance.

- **Location**

Next to the age range, you also need to specify the location where the ad will be shown. For most people, picking a place to publish ads to is easy. They just need to specify the serviceable area of their business. Facebook allows you to target people in a certain location. You can then use Google Maps to specify the location where your ads will show.

There are multiple ways for you to indicate the geographical location where you want to show your ads. The easiest way is to indicate the name of the city, town, state or country in the location field. You just need to type the name of the location and select the correct one from the suggestions of places that drops down. You may also add multiple different locations to the list so your ads would show in more than one place on the map.

If you choose to use this method, the ads will be shown to users within the border of the location you indicated. This method is effective when you are targeting users from a specific town, city or even an entire country. The geographical boundaries of these locations become the limits of the location where your ads will be shown.

Another way to pinpoint the location is by dropping a location pin on the map. You can zoom in and out of the map to place the pin accurately. After placing the location pin on the map, you then have the option to choose the radius of the circle that you want for your ad targeting. If you choose 10 miles for example, your ad will be shown in a 10 mile location from the location of the pin.

This method is better suited if you are targeting people in the vicinity of a specific place. If you have a store for example, you could put the pin on the location of your store on the map. You could then assign a targeting radius of 3 miles. Your ads will be shown to Facebook users within a 3-mile radius from your store. This kind of targeting makes more sense for small businesses because they are able to target the people near them. These people are more likely to become customers.

You can show your ad to any location on the globe where there are Facebook users. If you are managing the advertising for an international brand, you can use Facebook ads to attract users to a website or an app.

You can use the ads to attract users that your marketing would not be able to reach otherwise with the use of traditional advertising.

This is particularly useful if you are selling digital products or services. You will be able to show your digital wares to people who may have shown interest to similar products in the past. Even if your company is based in the US for example, you will be able to show your products to people in other countries where Facebook is also popular.

Facebook uses multiple location indicators to pinpoint the location of users. For mobile users, they may use the GPS on their phone to find out where the person is located. Desktop users on the other hand may be located using the location feature on the computer they are using. If they fall within the location that you indicated in your ad targeting, your ad can end up getting promoted their accounts.

- **Men vs Women**

You may also want to specify whether you want your ads shown solely to men or women. Ideally, you need to create a separate ad campaign for men and for women. Each sex has different interests and motivations for buying. They are also attracted to different ad creatives. Ad creatives refer to the visual aspect of the ad. It may include images and texts and the other visual elements that can be manipulated in the ad.

Even when advertising the same product to men and women, you will need to use a different ad campaign for each sex. Men are attracted to different colors and ad copies when compared to women. By targeting both sexes with the same set of ads, you are compromising between the two and this may make your ads less effective in attracting and converting people.

Detailed Targeting

While the age group and location of your audience will narrow down your ad target, it will still be too broad if you do not include other demographical information. Facebook allows you to target your audience even more accurately by allowing more filters in the Detailed Targeting section of the ad creation process. This section includes fields where you can add additional demographical information as well as target audience interest and behaviors.

To further boost the accuracy of your ads, you could type a characteristic of your target audience in the field provided. For instance, you may write the brand of a product that you are competing with. By targeting this specific brand, you will be able to show your ads to customers and the fans of your competitors.

If you are targeting mobile users only, you may specify the brand of phone that they are using. If you write the word iPhone in the field for example, you will find different options for targeting. They are usually labelled as "Interests", "Demographics" or "Behavior." They may also be labelled as a type of demographical information like "School", "Employer" or "Field of Study."

You could also choose to target people who own an iPhone 6, 7 or any other common types of iPhone. You may also target people who are generally interested in the iPhone as a subject. Interest means that they may have liked iPhone related content in the past. This could also mean that they reacted positively to pages, posts and comments related to iPhones. Your Detailed Targeting field will look like this:

INCLUDE people who match at least ONE of the following

Behaviors > Mobile Device User > All Mobile Devices by Brand > Apple

Owns: iPhone 7

Owns: iPhone 6

Following this example, your ad will be shown to Facebook users who own either an iPhone 7 or iPhone 6. This means that your ad will be shown to two groups of people. You could add more groups of people by adding more interest, behavior or demographical information in this field. The more you add to this list, the broader your target audience becomes.

The targeting information you include in these fields will be used together with the age group, sex and location information you entered previously to make further narrow down the audience of your ad. In Facebook Ad Manager, you will see an audience meter in the side of the screen that will indicate how narrow your targeting is. The meter will indicate if your <u>audience is too narrow, just right or too broad</u>. The information around the audience meter will also indicate how many people in your chosen location falls within your target audience.

If there are too few people to target (Narrow), the Facebook ads algorithm may not be able to deliver your ads. Your ad may just expire without getting a single impression or click. If the targeting is too broad on the other hand, your ads will be shown even to people who may not be interested in your product or service.

Use the audience meter to adjust your targeting information for your ad. A healthy target audience will make the audience meter pointer point on the green portion of the meter (Just Right).

If your targeting is too narrow, you can broaden it by adding more interests, behaviors or demographical information. You may also widen the age range and the location targeting of your ads.

If the targeting is too broad, however, you can also do the opposite. You could remove some of the interest, behavior and demographical targeting, as well as lessen the age range and the location radius.

Targeting a Subset of your Broad Audience (Narrowing Further)

You also have an option to target a part of a broader audience to further narrow your ads' audience. You can do this through the "Narrow Further" link in the bottom of the Detailed Targeting section of the ad editor. By using this feature, you will be able to target audiences using two or more interests. Let's say that you want to target iPhone users who are also Los Angeles Lakers fans. You could indicate the Los Angeles Lakers as an interest in the "INCLUDE people who match at least ONE of the following" field. You could then use the "Narrow Further" link to show the "and MUST ALSO match at least ONE of the following" field. You could use this field to target users who are using iPhone 6 and 7. In the end, your targeting fields will look something like this:

INCLUDE people who match at least ONE of the following

Interests > Additional Interests

  Los Angeles Lakers

and MUST ALSO match at least ONE of the following

Behaviors > Mobile Device User > All Mobile Devices by Brand > Apple

  Owns: iPhone 7

  Owns: iPhone 6

By using this kind of arrangement, you are targeting people who are interested in the Los Angeles Lakers (NBA team) and also owns an iPhone 7, an iPhone 6 or both phones. Your ad will not show to just any user who has shown interest towards the Los Angeles Lakers. They must also own the iPhones indicated in the targeting fields for the ads to show in their account.

With this feature, you are able to gain even more control over the people who see you ad. However, you also run the danger of making your targeting too narrow.

Excluding Groups of People

In the same line where you'll find the "Narrow Further" link, you will also see the "Exclude People" link. This way, you can choose to exclude people who have specific interests and behaviors. You can also pick more than one characteristic to identify the people that you want to exclude.

Budget and Duration

After setting the target information for your ads, the next step is to set your budget and the running duration for your Facebook ad campaign. The right budget will vary depending on the location where you want to show your ads and the general competition level in that location. You will also need a bigger budget if you are advertising in a location where many other people and businesses are advertising. If you are the only person advertising in a particular place on the other hand, you can get by with a budget as low as $5 per day.

Aside from the competition from other advertisers, your budget will also be affected by the goal of your advertising campaign. If you only want to get post impressions or page likes, $5 per day is enough to get a decent amount of views in a location with low competition. If you want to drive traffic to a website on the other hand, you will need to assess the cost per click on your ad to know the exact amount that you will need to get a decent amount of views. Luckily, you will be able to adjust your demographical information to try to decrease the cost per click of your campaign. To achieve this however, there will be plenty of trial and error.

Facebook makes the financial side of your campaign transparent even before you start it. When setting a budget for instance, the Facebook ad editor will tell you how much money you will need for your ad to run for the duration you specify. You can adjust your daily ad budget and the duration to have control over the overall spending of the campaign.

You also have the option to run the ad campaign continuously. You just need to set a daily budget for the ad and it will continue to run until you manually stop it. Be careful with this setting though because this will lead to a monthly deduction from your credit card. If you forget that you have a Facebook ad running, you may be surprised by the ad campaign amounts on your credit card bill.

After setting up the ad budget and duration, the next step is to add a payment option for your ad campaign. The available payment options vary per country. The most commonly used mode of payment are credit cards and debit cards. If you choose to use a card, Facebook will do a test transaction on it to make sure that it is still active. If the transaction is successful, you will be able to start your promotion. Otherwise, you will need to add another mode of payment that Facebook can verify.

Refining your ad targeting

You cannot expect to get your desired results after just one Facebook ad campaign. By researching in advance, you may be able to experience some level of success. However, you will always find points where you can further improve your ad's performance. You can do this by adjusting the targeting mechanism of your ads.

An example of this is by targeting different age groups with your ads. You can create three different ad campaigns where the difference is the age group. One campaign may target 21-25 year-olds with the second and third campaigns targeting the 26-30 and 31-35 age groups respectively. If all other characteristics aside from the age group are similar, you will be able to compare the effectiveness of your ad according to the age group.

The general goal when refining your targeting data is to minimize the cost of advertising. Targeting issues will lead to a low conversion rate. In Facebook, conversion rate is calculated by the number of conversions (desired outcome) divided by the impressions (the number of times an ad is shown). The result is then multiplied by 100% to convert it to percent. The lower your conversion rate, the more expensive the ad campaign becomes. Most of the time, a low conversion rate is a result of poor targeting.

You can further improve the performance and efficiency of the ad by experimenting on different changes on the targeting of the ads. Your goal is to find a group of people that you can convert but aren't targeted by other marketers in your niche market.

Chapter Five: The Facebook Sales Funnel

Your Facebook ad campaign will only be successful if you are aware of the part of the sales funnel that your audience is currently in. The Facebook sales funnel differs from the sales funnels you have seen in the past and this is due to the way people use the Facebook platform. Here's how the Facebook sales funnel works:

1. Brand Awareness

Brand awareness happens when the Facebook user becomes aware that your brand exists. It could also happen when the user discovers that your real world business can also be found on Facebook. There are multiple ways to create brand awareness on Facebook. Most brands use content marketing to achieve this. Content marketing is generally considered an organic marketing method. However, on Facebook, you can use the Boost promotion feature to increase the reach and overall effectiveness of your content.

Using boosted content is a common strategy on Facebook. For instance, you could write a blog post on your company blog about promotions that you think your potential customers will care about. You could then share this on your Facebook page. Link posts on Facebook, however, perform poorly when compared to images and videos. To make sure that more people see it, you can choose to boost it while also targeting your potential customers. This will expose your brand to more Facebook users, creating brand awareness.

Video content is an even better medium for brand awareness because of the auto-play feature of the Facebook ads. Just like the link content above, you can also boost video content to make sure it shows in the newsfeeds of your target audience. The key to increasing engagement of video content in Facebook is by creating a strong introduction. The first five seconds of a video will determine whether the Facebook user will continue watching of skip it.

The downside of using video is that it can be difficult to create if you have no prior experience on video marketing. If you choose to use this type of media, you may need to hire someone with experience on video editing or you could find a professional to do the video making for you.

2. Initial Engagement

Brand awareness is a passive step in the sales funnel. It happens when the user sees your page on Facebook. Not all first encounters, however, will lead to engagement. For the Facebook user to move to the next step of the sales funnel, he or she needs to engage with your brand. As mentioned earlier in the book, there are multiple ways for your users to engage with your content. The most passive methods of engagement are clicked reactions. Images, status updates and videos generally get a lot of "likes", "loves" and "lol" from the Facebook audience. Getting a lot of positive reactions from users will improve the visibility (impressions) of your posts.

Comments have an even greater impact on your content's visibility. Posts that have a higher number of comments tend to get more impressions. Not all popular posts get a lot of comments, of course. To make sure that people make comments on your posts, you could experiment with using engaging language in the posts that you boost. For instance, add a question on the description of one of your popular posts. Adding a question will make more users interact more with your content.

Some types of posts can become comment magnets when they are boosted at the right time. For instance, you could post something like this and boost it:

Happy Birthday to Us!

Coffee shop ABCD is celebrating our 5th year anniversary. Greet us congratulations and get a chance to win a large cup of the coffee flavor of your choice.

This kind of promotional post, when boosted at the right time, will become a comment magnet. Certain types of comments, like "congratulations" significantly increase the visibility of your posts. People who like your page will see this type of post at the top spot of their newsfeed when they load their app or when they log in.

3. Fandom

Fandom happens when people who constantly like or comment on your posts start to follow your page. If they choose to like your page, they are more likely to see your posts every time they log into the network.

Getting likes alone, you must note, is no longer enough. In the past, fans will always see your post even if you don't boost them. However, because of the changes in Facebook's algorithm and the increased competition among business pages in the network, it is now much harder to get your posts to your intended audience without the help of promotions.

Boosting is one way for you to increase the visibility of your posts. However, boosting *will only increase the visibility of your posts*. Not all boosted posts will get the right amount of engagement that's enough to make it viral. You need to make sure that the type of content you boost are attention-catching and engaging.

Aside from boosting your posts, you can also create a Facebook Group for your fans to make sure that those who are loyal to your brand will immediately see your content. If a Facebook Group is active and gets a lot of engagement, the contents shared in it will be shown to its members.

When a Facebook user likes your page and constantly interacts with the content you post, they are more likely to buy your product. These users are more open to learning what your product and business is about. Some of them may even order your product if given a chance.

To make this first sale, you could create promotions that are exclusive to your Facebook fans. By giving away discounts or giveaways, you are rewarding your fans for taking part in your Facebook community.

Fans are also more open to clicking on links that lead to a website outside of the Facebook network. You can encourage fans to go to your website through content marketing and by creating interactive activities in your website. If your website has a forum feature for instance, constantly remind your fans that they could go there if they have questions or customer service concerns. You may also post blog entries regularly, featuring willing fans on them and sharing them on Facebook.

4. Conversion

Conversion happens when the Facebook users you interact with using ads and posts become actual customers. There are many types of conversion, depending on the type of action that you want your audience to do. A store may associate conversion to sales, while a non-profit organization may associate it with donations and volunteerism.

For your Facebook ad campaign to become successful, you need to define what the ultimate conversion is like for your organization. You want to keep the conversion task in mind whenever you start a campaign. Keep in mind the action that you want your users to do. By starting with the end in mind, you will be able to define who your likely target audience are and how you can better target them.

Conversion is the end goal of all ad campaigns. By focusing on how you can convert your target audience, you will be able to avoid the common mistake of going after unimportant numbers like impressions and likes. Getting a high amount of impressions and likes will not amount to anything if your ad campaigns do not lead to conversions.

Knowing what your conversion task will also help you in crafting the best ad copy. You will be able to choose the correct message to use in order to attract users and convince them to convert.

5. Remarketing

Remarketing is the process of reaching out to people who have made contact with your brand in the past. Through the use of ads, you can remarket content and promotional posts towards users who follow and like your page, has made comments on your posts and even people who visited your website in the past.

Using Facebook Pixel, you will be able to track Facebook users who visit your website. With this tool, you'll find multiple ways through which you can encourage fans and non-fans alike to visit your website again to make a purchase.

Facebook Pixel is a tracking technology provided by Facebook to advertisers to allow them to track the movement of users in their websites. You can set up a Facebook Pixel code in your website and similar to the other analytic tracking codes. When a Facebook user goes to your website, their visit is logged in their account. You could track them throughout your website as long as the page they visit has a Facebook Pixel code in it.

One effective technique for remarketing is to add Facebook Pixel codes in the last page of the purchasing package (ecommerce cart) and the thank you page after the purchase. By putting two separate codes here, you will be able to track how many people from Facebook completed a sale. You will also be able to track how many of the users went as far as the checkout page before abandoning their cart.

Creating your Own Sales Funnel

Now that you know what the Facebook sales funnel looks like, it's time to create your own, based on your business or organizational goals. You can begin by first understanding your target users:

1. **Learn the current behaviors and interests of your users**

The key to an effective Facebook ad campaign is knowing who your target audience is. You would want to do a thorough research on who they are and how they behave. One way to go about this is by looking at your current Facebook friends and making smart guesses on who among them may be interested in buying your product.

You can also hold a Facebook poll. You can start polls in Facebook pages, groups and in Messenger. In the poll, you can ask your friends directly who among them are interested in buying your product or your service.

List down the people who answered the poll positively and make note of their common characteristics. You can also look at their accounts for clues about their behavior in the network. For instance, you could try to identify the types of content that they like, comment on and share. You could also check the time when they are most active on Facebook.

Focus on the information that you can also use in your initial targeting. Find demographical information that are common among these people. You could then run a test ad using the behaviors and interest that you get from your simple survey.

2. Find ways to disrupt their usual behaviors

All of your potential customers or clients will come from Facebook. You will need to accept that they aren't usually in a buying mood when they are browsing through the social network. Instead, they are more focused on simply killing time.

You will need to disrupt this usual behavior using a combination of ads and content marketing. The right type of content will get their attention while the advertising process will ensure that your content will actually reach your target audience.

To disrupt the usual routine of your target Facebook users, test out different types of marketing styles. Here are some of the techniques you can try:

- Free trials
- Freebies
- Special Promotions
- Event invitations
- Contests

These are examples of techniques that you can use to get people's attention. Choose the particular types of promotional styles that will allow your users to test out the process that you want them to continue doing in the future.

An ecommerce website that is newly introduced to the Facebook community can give away freebies that can only be processed using the ecommerce website's shopping cart. By investing in such a promotion, the ecommerce website can also put their purchasing system to the test. You could also make them pay for the shipping of the freebies so that you can record their payment information in the system. By giving out a few freebies, you can allow some of your fans to engage with your website and go through the purchasing process.

3. Target Lookalike Audiences

By using Facebook Pixels, you also target unique groups of Facebook users called Lookalike Audiences. Using Facebook Pixels data, Facebook can target people with similar characteristics to those who visit your website. By putting a unique Facebook Pixel code in the Thank You page of your shopping cart for example, you can use the Pixel data to target other potential buyers of your product. Lookalike audiences will give you the option to reach out to people outside of your fan base who have similar characteristics of your buyers.

You also have the option to target lookalike audiences using a collection of your Facebook fans. However, if you are looking for conversion, you will get better performing ads with data from Facebook Pixels.

Chapter Six: Creating an Ad Copy That Works

Now that you know how the average Facebook ad is structures, you need to start thinking of what kind of message you want to send your target audience. The general goal is to make the Facebook users click on the link. Because Facebook ads are designed to look like the average Facebook post (Native Advertising), and most of the time, people may not even be aware that they are clicking on an ad.

The character limit is usually the biggest challenge that most beginner advertisers face. It is difficult to create an effective copy with a 90-character limit. You'll also won't know how effective the copy will be unless you actually test them out with the market.

To help you think of a copy for your first campaigns, here are some Facebook ad copy techniques you can try:

- Use the word "You" and its variation

The word "You" is powerful in getting the attention of target users. Here are some examples of ad descriptions that use the pronoun:

You don't need to work three jobs to buy that dream house. Find the perfect job today.

- An ad description for a Job Ad Website

Your family depends on you. Who are you depending on?

- Description for an Insurance Ad

• Use Action Words in the Image

Action words refer to words that tell your users what to do. You audiences are likely to read whatever is written in the image first before reading the header or the description of the ad posting. Here is an example of a short but effective sentence that uses an action word:

Get a 30% discount on your first purchase using our new app!

Build your online store before noon today!

Don't be a hoarder. Sell your stuff on SellYourTrash.com

• Use Creative One-liners

Because you have a limited number of characters to work with for your Facebook ads, you will need make use of one-liner catch phrases to grab people's attention. Many ads go straight to the point by asking people to buy or to sign up. You can make your ads stand out by thinking of one liners that easily catch people's attention.

You can put a one-liner phrase in the beginning of the description or in the image of the post. If people are interested, they will check out both parts of your ad.

- Ask a Question

Question marks are proven to work when it comes to getting people's attention. Whenever a question mark enters our peripheral vision, we immediately look at the question that comes with it to see if it concerns us. This is why you should learn to ask engaging questions on your Facebook ads. Ideally, you want to put your questions together with your image. You could also make the meta title of your link into a question. The link's meta title also takes up a lot of space in your content.

- Include figures (discounts, percentages, etc.)

People love numbers especially if it is together with the words like discount. If you are offering discounts, make sure to add the maximum amount that they can save if they avail of it.

In this case, include the bigger figure into your ad. If the item for sale costs $1,000 for example, and you have 20% off, you will attract more people of they see that they will save $200. Instead of saying:

"Save up to 20% off"

Say this instead:

"Save up to $200 on your next purchase"

$200 looks like a bigger figure than 20% even though both figures have the same value. The bigger the savings amount on paper, the more effective the ad becomes in attracting people.

- Keep your Offer simple and straight to the point

When thinking of creative ways to present an ad, marketers often make the mistake of forgetting the call to action. Just to be safe, write a short call to action first. Write the ad call to action and as well as the offer that aims to convince the user to take the action. After that, look for ways to shorter the statement. This way, you will have more space for the other content of your ad.

Remember to make the offer short, simple and easy to understand. Use language that people are familiar with such as discount, clearance sales or promos. If you are in need of inspiration for short but effective offers, look around the ads on Google. The ads on these networks have an even shorter character limit.

- Align your description, image text and call-to-action

It is also important to keep your content consistent throughout the ad. Keep your message consistent from the description, the text image and the call to action button. The Facebook user must be able to understand what the offer is even if they are just looking at the image or the description.

Chapter Seven: Secrets to Facebook Ads Success

The true secret to making a successful ad campaign lies in your knowledge about your audience. Constantly ask yourself this question:

What will make may target audience take action?

If you can answer this question accurately, you will be able to apply your insight into creating effective ads.

- Limit the use of colors in the image, but add an accent color to grab attention

While bright colors are effective in attracting attention, people will hate your ad if there are too many bright colors. Try to limit the amount of colors in the image you use to three. If possible, use the bright color as an accent that will make the image more memorable. Click bait pages employ this strategy by putting a red arrow or circle on the image. Our eyes are naturally attracted to these images.

- Include branding on the image

If you are selling a popular brand, make the brand name and logo recognizable in the image of the ad. This will catch the attention of brand conscious buyers. Remember that you can only do this if you actually have the rights to represent the brand. Otherwise, Facebook will take down your ad should the original brand company complain about your ad.

- Use images that are relevant to the interest of your target audience

The image takes up the biggest space in your post and is also the thing that grabs people's attention. It only makes sense that you use an image that would engage your target audience. You will know if your image is compelling enough through the engagement-impression percentage of your ad. If less than 5% of your impressions result to an engagement, you need to adjust your image and text content to grab more attention from the users.

- Use stock photos with smiling actors

Having people in the ad photos have been proven to attract people's attention. A photo with a smiling person in it is even more effective when compared to ones without them.

Aside from smiles, also experiment on using images of people who look directly towards the camera. When Facebook users see these images, they are naturally drawn to it. It fools the users' mind into thinking that there is someone looking in his or her direction.

- Make use of relevant holidays and important events that matter to your users

Facebook usage increases during holidays when there is no school or work. Take advantage of this by reaching out to the audience who are resting from work or school. A bar for example, could create ads right before and during St. Patrick's Day. Companies around the stadium during Superbowl could create ads and promotions related to the event. This shows that your company is a part of the community and it may lead to better loyalty from people who are passionate about the event.

Chapter Eight: Creating a Landing Page for your Facebook Ads

After people click on your Facebook ads, you have the option to direct them to a destination outside of the Facebook platform. The page where they will be directed to is called the *landing page*.

The landing page is just as important as the ad copies you create. It should contain the necessary content and features that will encourage the users to complete the objective of your ad campaign.

Landing Page Characteristics

The landing page differs from other types of webpages on your website. An ideal landing page is free from distractions. To do this, create a page that is free of unnecessary links. An ordinary webpage for example, has a link to the home page at the top and a list of important links on the website's top bar. These features may be removed to make the landing page more effective.

You may further remove distractions from the landing page by eliminating any ads from the page. Ads, even the ones for your own company, distracts the user from the goal of the Facebook ad campaign.

By removing any ad that is not related to the objective of the Facebook ad campaign, you will be able to prevent users from doing any unintended actions on your landing page.

When you have removed all the possible distractions from your landing page, the users will then be limited to only a few actions. When a user closes the page immediately after clicking on an ad, the action is called a bounce.

Why do people bounce off of your landing page?

People usually bounce when they did not expect to be directed to a landing page. A small percentage of the people who bounce off your landing page are accidental clickers. In most cases, it is the responsibility of Facebook's ad team to track these accidental clicks and deduct it from your total bill.

Sometimes, users also bounce off your page when the contents of the landing page were not as they expected. If your Facebook ads indicated that you are giving away free stuff, but your landing page does not say anything about the freebie, there is a good chance that your users will bounce.

Landing Page Objectives

To prevent this from happening, the content of your ads need to be aligned with the contents of your landing page. The contents of your landing page need to be a continuation of the call-to-action button of your ad. If your ad talks about signing up for your business' newsletter for example, your first paragraph on the landing page need to be related to that action. By doing so, you are connecting the experience from the Facebook ad to your landing page.

Encouraging your users to engage with the content

Aside from bouncing, the only other option for the user is to read or listen to the content on the page. This is what you want people to do. Use the contents above the fold to hook them in. You can do this by using copywriting techniques discussed in earlier chapters. Techniques like asking questions and using numerical data can hook the users into reading further. Experiment on the different techniques suggested above and stick with the most effective ones.

Creating the call-to-action

All the contents of your page page must be directed towards one objective. As mentioned above, the objective of the landing page needs to be aligned with the objective of your Facebook ad.

The call-to-action is a landing page feature that will initiate the process that you want the audience to go through. If the objective of the ad campaign is to get more sales, the call-to-action button needs to initiate the sales process. In this case, the button could say "Buy Now" or "Check Prices".

These action words are usually put inside a button or big text links. It should be obvious to the user that the words can be clicked. The wording of the call-to-action feature also needs to be clear and straight to the point. They need to know what will happen next if they actually clicked on the link.

The call-to-action feature may also contain other parts aside from the button. If the goal of the campaign is to schedule more appointments for your business, you may want to include a scheduling tool where the users can enter their contact details so that your representatives can call them back. In this case, you will need an additional field in your call-to-action feature where they could enter their phone number or their email address.

Directing Attention towards the Call-to-Action feature

If your call-to-action feature is ready, you need to adjust all the other parts of your landing page to make sure that the user's attention naturally flow towards it. You need to do this through the use of the contents of the page.

Text content is the easiest type to create. Almost all online pages have some sort of text content. In fact, your users will be expecting some text content on the landing page to tell them about it and what they should do next. It's only fitting that you put text content as the header of the page, at the first paragraph above the fold.

It's easier to make people from Facebook engage with text content because it requires minimal commitment from them. The visitors of your landing page will be able to see how long the paragraph is, so they will be able to assess how much time they need to read through it. Unlike video or audio content, they do not need to click on anything to get started with engaging with text content. Because of this, using text content is one of the most effective ways to start your landing page content.

People, however, often lose interest when they see that the page only contains text. They are used to interactive pages that contain a lot of visual features. To hook your users into reading the text content, make use of headers and special fonts. Using attention grabbing fonts and headers is effective in attracting the attention of the user to a certain part of the page. However, this strategy should be used selectively because overusing it could lead to your landing page looking like a spam page.

Aside from using headers and special fonts, you could also use images to break the monotony of your text content. Add one image for every two or three paragraphs on your page. This will make your landing page easier to read and more pleasing to the eyes.

Do make sure that all the images on your landing page needs are connected to the objective of the page. If your landing page's objective is to sell more products for example, use images of people directly using the product. You may also include images of the product shot from different angles. This will show the users how the product looks when it arrives.

On the other hand, if you want users to visit your brick-and-mortar shop, use images of your shop. When talking about the location of the shop for example, use a map image to show the users the different landmarks around your shop. If they are familiar with the area, the map will allow them to make pinpoint the exact of the location of your shop.

You can also use images of the exterior and the interior of your shop. This will allow them to become familiar with the place even before they go there. You could also add an image of the receiving area of your shop, together with a smiling employee. Putting a person in the image makes your overall landing page more relatable to the users.

To make your call-to-action feature stand out, make it bigger than most of the content in your landing page. Arrange the images and the text so that a reader's attention flows naturally towards the call to action. One way to do this is by putting the call-to-action link directly after the paragraph. The text content on the paragraph should then talk about why the users should click on the link.

Adding video content to your landing page

Video content will also make your landing page more exciting for the users. If done properly, it will improve user engagement and increase the time they spend on your page. Just like the text and the image contents though, your video content should also serve a specific purpose in relation to the objective of the ad campaign. Some of the common purpose of video content in the landing page are:

1. To communicate with the user directly

Videos allow you or any member of your organization to communicate with the audience directly. By talking to the audience directly, you can increase the chances of your message getting through. If the video is captured and edited properly, it will make the landing page feel more like a personal encounter. In contrast, most landing pages feel like reading an ad. Communicating to the audience through the video will help in making the ad campaign experience less like a business transaction.

2. To convince them why they should go through the call to action

Generally, the audience of your landing page is more likely to go through the objective task of the campaign if you explain the benefits through a video. In contrast, they are more likely to scan through a text list. By recording yourself explaining the benefits of going through the process, you will also be able to increase the comprehension of the message of the landing page.

3. To explain complicated instructions in a short period

Lastly, if your objective requires the users to go through a complicated process, it may be easier for your users to understand if they watch a video that explains the process. The video can be helpful for users who aren't familiar with the process. This includes first time customers and elderly users.

Arranging Your Content

The arrangement of the content on your landing page also needs to follow the reading direction of the user. In general, English language readers start reading from the upper left side of the page. You can put the header of the landing page in this part of your page, readily letting the reader know what the content is about.

The header needs to be followed with an introductory paragraph. By the time the user arrives at your landing page, they will already have an idea about the objective of your ad campaign based on the call-to-action on your Facebook ad. As stated previously in the chapter, your landing page will be more effective if the first paragraph is aligned with the call to action phrase in your ad.

After your opening paragraph, all the other contents in your page need to focus on convincing the user to go through the objective task. Here are some of the information you can add to encourage this:

- List the benefits of performing the requested action

With this type of information, you tell the users what they will get if they go through with buying a product or setting up an appointment. If you are selling something with your ad campaign, people will want to know what they are getting for the amount that they are paying.

Most users will base their decision to go through with the process on this information. If the benefits of your offer significantly outweighs the price, people are more likely to take it.

- Testimonials of other customers

Testimonials work as social proof that the offer is truly beneficial to the users. Positive testimonials lets the user know that your product or service has been tested by others before and with positive results.

- Positive reviews from authoritative sources

Positive reviews, just like testimonials, also act as social proof that your offer can satisfy the user's needs. Reviews may also come with additional visual features like a five-star rating system. Made popular by ecommerce websites like Amazon, online users often use these rating systems to help them make purchasing decisions.

- Images of the product, service or location of the business

The right type of images will also help in convincing people to go through with your objective task. If the ad is meant to sell a physical product, it's better if you provide a 360 degree image of the product you are selling.

- Information about the important people related to the business

If you are selling a service, there may also be a need to include information about the people employed to do the service. It will be easier to convince other people to sign up for a service if they know that the people who are running the business are professionals. A bit of history about the business and the people behind it all contribute positively.

For example, if you are selling a book then it would help if you include information about the author. For instance, you may include the titles of other books written by the same author.

Appealing to people's emotions

By including facts about the product and the business in your landing page, you are appealing to the logical side of the potential customer. You can go even further towards increasing the success rate of your landing page by appealing to their emotional side.

There are multiple emotions that you can channel in your landing page sales copy to make people take action. The most common example would be the use of happiness as a lure to buy the product. Many companies like Coca Cola and McDonald's use this in their commercials. For example, Coca Cola usually surrounds their products with smiling friends and family members. They may even release holiday ads during Thanksgiving and Christmas. By doing so, they are programming people's minds to associate their product with happy moments and occasions.

Satisfaction is another emotional state that businesses love to use in their advertisements. For instance, toothpaste ads love to emphasize the refreshing feeling that you get from their product after brushing your teeth. By using imagery like sparkling teeth, menthol and ice, they are able to make the audience remember the satisfaction one gets after brushing their teeth.

Comedy can also be used to make a landing page more memorable. If people laugh at some parts of your landing page, they are more likely to remember its content. By including some timely jokes in the content of your landing page, you will be able to make use of comedy as a memory tools. The joke will be even more effective if it is related to the product or service that you are presenting in the page.

Fear and worry. If none of the positive emotional experiences work for your product or service, you may also use fear as a motivator for buying. In fact, many experts suggest that fear and the state of being worried is one of the best purchasing motivators out there.

There are many ways for you to create this sense of fear through your landing page. For instance, you can say that the product is of limited supply or a certain promotion has a time limit. This creates a feeling of fear that they may miss out on the product or the service that you are offering. It also creates an artificial sense of urgency among the audiences of your landing page.

For products and services related to health, health scares can be used to push the audience into buying a product or a service. This is especially useful if the product or service that you are offering prevents bad health conditions.

However, do make sure that you avoid abusing these themes in your content. Too much of it can actually turn a potential client away.

Conclusion

Creating effective Facebook ads is certainly a skill that you'll have to master as you go. You need to give yourself the opportunity to practice and even make mistakes to be good at it. The good news is that the learning curve isn't all that steep as long as you know what to watch out for.

Now that you're equipped with essential information, go over to your Facebook business page and start thinking of your first ad campaign. Explore the different types of ads that you can create and start thinking of ad copies that would work on your organization's goal.

Remember to start by creating a goal and then listing the characteristics of the users that you want to target. You can even try to set up an ad campaign just to experience how it is done. This will get you familiarized with how things work so that when you're ready for the real thing, it's a lot less nerve-wracking to do.

Also, it is always best to start small when planning for your budget. Start with a $1-$5 budget per week. Don't be afraid to terminate the ad campaign if it's starting to eat up too much of your budget, but is not producing any real results. This only means that there are things that you still need to adjust in your targeting setting.

Lastly, always learn from your mistakes. All of us make mistakes when we create ad campaigns for the first time. The ones who do succeed are those who are able to learn from their mistakes and keep on improving their technique.

www.ingramcontent.com/pod-product-compliance
Lightning Source LLC
Chambersburg PA
CBHW071439210326
41597CB00020B/3864